D1283215

Why Children Should Know Their Grandparents

by

The Association of Black Cardiologists Inc.

Featuring Illustrations
by Joel Gresham

Publishing Associates, Inc. • Atlanta, Georgia

Mission of the Association of Black Cardiologists, Inc.:

We believe that good health is the cornerstone of progress. We are firm in our resolve to make exemplary health care accessible and affordable to all in need, dedicated to the elimination of disparities in the prevalence, quality health care and manpower in cardiovascular diseases. We are guided by high ethics in all transactions and strive for excellence in our training and skills.

This is our entire reason for being!

ABC welcomes your tax-deductible contributions and gifts to maintain and support our advocacy, our publications, our research and volunteer programs for our churches, our schools, our beauty shops and barber shops, our work places, and our medical institutions. Through your volunteer efforts and your contributions, we hope you will join ABC in lowering the high rate of cardiovascular disease in our community.

Contact the ABC for details on how you can help!
1-800-753-9222

B. Waine Kong, Ph.D, J.D.
Chief Executive Officer
Association of Black Cardiologists, Inc.
6849-B2 Peachtree Dunwoody Road, N.E. Atlanta, GA 30328
bwainekong@abcardio.org
www.abcardio.org

Published by Publishing Associates, Inc. 5020 Montcalm Drive Atlanta, GA 30331
ISBN: 0942683-41-2 A library quality trade publication

Table of Contents

Table of Contents (cont.'d.)

We are All Somebody's Grandchild!

Children Should Know Their Grandparents

When a grandparent dies, an entire library goes up in flames. So why are so many of our African American 'libraries' being destroyed prematurely? These 'libraries' are being destroyed by heart disease, stroke and diabetes. If we want stable neighborhoods where children are polite, we need grandparents. Children readily resist their parents but think twice about upsetting Grandma and Grandpa.

If you love your children, you will want to live long enough to love their children as well. When a flight attendant announces safety instructions, it's "In case of emergency, put the oxygen mask on yourself first." If you are not conscious, you cannot help anyone. So, if you want to be around for those special people in the future—take care of yourself first.

This book is a tribute to the special relationship between grandparents and children... you and your grandchildren. Just as there is no way to explain the color red to a blind person, only by becoming a grandparent (when one actually holds a grandchild) can the magic of being a grandparent be realized. This is best described by a grandmother who said if she had known having grandchildren was so much fun, she would have had them first. When you take better care of yourself, everyone benefits.

We invite you to share these images with your grandchildren. They were lovingly created by world renowned artist, Mr. Joel Gresham, with you in mind. We also invite you to share your own grandparents story for inclusion in a future ABC publication, or as a testimonial that will appear on our website. Contact us at: www.abcardio.org. Taking charge of your health is the best way to give your family a future as well as a heritage. They will only have a bright future if you are in it. And don't forget to celebrate Grandparents Day... the first Sunday after Labor Day!

National Grandparents Day

By the President of the United States of America

A Proclamation

As we seek to strengthen the enduring values of the family, it is appropriate that we honor our grandparents.

Grandparents are our continuing tie to the near-past, to the events and beliefs and experiences that so strongly affect our lives and the world around us. Whether they are our own or surrogate grandparents who fill some of the gaps in our mobile society, our senior generation also provides our society a link to our national heritage and traditions.

We all know grandparents whose values transcend passing fads and pressures, and who possess the wisdom of distilled pain and joy. Because they are usually free to love and guide and befriend the young without having to take daily responsibility for them, they can often reach out past pride and fear of failure and close the space between generations.

The Congress, by joint resolution (H.J. Res. 244), has authorized and requested the President to designate the first Sunday of September following Labor Day of each year as National Grandparents Day.

NOW, THEREFORE, I, JIMMY CARTER, President of the United States of America, do hereby designate Sunday, September 9, 1979 and the first Sunday following Labor Day in each succeeding year as "National Grandparents Day."

I urge officials of Government at the national, State, and local levels, and of voluntary organizations to plan appropriate activities that recognize the importance and the worth of the 17 million grandparents in our nation. I urge all Americans to take the time to honor their own grandparents or those in their community.

IN WITNESS WHEREOF, I have hereunto set my hand this sixth day of September, in the year of our Lord nineteen hundred seventy-nine, and of the Independence of the United States of America the two hundred and fourth.

Jimmy Carter

Mrs. Marian McQuade began a campaign in 1970 to set aside a day for grandparents. Her efforts led to the creation and the official proclamation of Grandparents Day by President Jimmy Carter on September 9, 1979.

Grandparents Day is celebrated each year the first Sunday of September following Labor Day.

Marian McQuade and her husband Joe are the parents of 15 children. They have 40 grandchildren, and eight great-grandchildren.

As Grandparents Day approaches, help Children and/or Grandchildren to identify and date all photos in old family albums. Many happy memories can be derived from this. Everyone is a grandchild and can be involved in the observance of this day -- a time to discover one's roots and learn patience, understanding and appreciation for the elderly. Grandparents Day is a perfect time to enhance communication between the generations.

Grandparents are a national treasure and resource. If we are ever going to solve our social problems, we need grandparents to live longer, healthier lives. We need grandparents to be available to their grandchildren. A community free of juvenile delinquency, adolescent and unwanted pregnancies, school drop out and underachievement, as well as a host of other issues that plague our community can only be achieved with lots and lots of grandparents. A child is only a grandparent away from developing into happy, well adjusted, contributing members of society. There's authority that children respect.

These national treasures are leaving us way too soon. The problem is, due to heart disease, diabetes and stroke, too many grandparents leave us even before their grand-children arrive. This is the thief that is robbing African American children of their grandparents.

Cardiovascular disease kills more than half of all grandparents—more than all other causes of death, combined.

Cardiovascular disease is a lifestyle problem. How we live causes this tremendous loss of lives. It is not dramatic breakthroughs in medicine that will make a difference in our life expectancy and quality of life. This can only come about when we decide to take responsibility for our health and prevent the disease before it wreaks havoc.

Cardiovascular disease is preventable. If we follow the *Seven Steps to a Healthy Heart* promoted by the Association of Black Cardiologists, Inc., we can prevent heart disease, diabetes and stroke and live long enough to love our grandchildren.

1. **Be Spiritually Active**
2. **Take Charge of Your Blood Pressure**
3. **Control Your Cholesterol**
4. **Track Your Blood Sugar**
5. **Enjoy Regular Exercise, Eat Smart and Manage Your Weight**
6. **Don't Smoke**
7. **Access Better Healthcare**

Children who have nurturing grandparents may get tripped or even stumble, but they will never hit the ground.

While other children can look forward to a lifetime of nurturing from their grandparents and great-grandparents, African American children cannot. By the time African American children graduate from high school, they are fortunate if they have one grandparent living, usually the grandmother. Only one out of four African American men live past the age of seventy-five. Cardiovascular disease is the cause of death of two out of four of them. And yet, we rise.

The journey on the road to happy, healthier, wealthier, well-adjusted lives starts with the first step. Life can be characterized as a journey up a mountain road. What we have done as a society is to develop a marvelous ambulance system, great hospitals, superb physicians and surgeons, nurses that care, medicines that work predictably without unwanted side effects. Yet, just like all the king's horses and all the king's men couldn't put Humpty together again, as advanced as our medicine is, it will never be as good as preventing the problem in the first place. While improvements in medicine will always be celebrated, we should also install railings or barriers (preventive strategies) to keep us from falling over the precipice in the first place.

To prevent death from heart disease, we should follow the success of modern dentistry. It wasn't long ago that everyone expected to be fitted for dentures by forty years old. Denture manufacturers dotted the landscape. Then science taught us that tooth decay could be avoided if we followed just three rules.

(1) Brush and floss our teeth twice per day (Lifestyle).
(2) Fluoridate our drinking water (Public Policy).
(3) See a dentist twice per year for check-ups (Clinical Practice).

As a result, tooth decay is no longer a problem for 90% of Americans. Thanks to the collective efforts of the American Dental Association, the National Dental Association, the US Public Health Service, schools and the media, today most people under the age of 40 years old have never had a toothache.

It turns out that tooth decay is a preventable problem and one can now expect to live a long life with the same set of teeth that they grew in at seven years old.

Did you know that each year more than a million Americans die from heart disease? Even worse, African Americans die from heart disease and stroke at a 50% higher rate than other Americans. Did you also know that heart disease, diabetes and stroke kill more African Americans than cancer, accidents, pneumonia, AIDS, diabetes, liver failure, suicide, homicide and all other causes of death combined?

Even if you don't die from heart disease, diabetes or stroke, it can still spoil the quality of your life. As many as half of all African Americans living today will eventually suffer a debilitating illness from a disease of the heart and blood vessels.

It ought not be. There is a lot you can do to help prevent heart disease, by getting regular health check-ups, eating right, and staying active.

This book assumes that you are already steering clear of practices that are extremely unhealthy or even suicidal. For example, you don't overindulge in alcohol or take illegal drugs. You don't misuse firearms, and when you are in a car, you buckle your seat belt. You look both ways before crossing the street.

Maybe you also seek medical care immediately when you have a health problem. And maybe you always follow your doctor's advice and prescription. But do you also know the importance of good preventive care? Are you aware of your glucose, A1C, blood pressure, and cholesterol values? When was the last time you had a check-up or examined your diet and exercise routine?

Growing older doesn't have to bring health worries, dependency, or limitations on your activities. By taking steps to prevent cardiovascular disease, you can live longer and have an active, fulfilling life at any age.

Use this step-by-step program to set goals that will help you thrive. Discuss your goals with your health care provider, and record your progress.

Your efforts and your successes will inspire others in your family and community toward healthier living. So, start setting the right example. African American children deserve to know their grandparents. Together, our families and our communities deserve a brighter, healthier future. Think of your body as a temple, and care for it as something precious and irreplaceable.

Now is the time to take the right steps.

The ABC is grateful to the contributors on this project for their collaborative efforts.

Ms. LaTrese Coyt	Mr. Joel Gresham
B. Waine Kong, Ph.D, JD	Jesse E. McGee, MD
Mr. Rondereo Sidney	Paul Underwood, MD

Parents give children what they need;
Grandparents give them what they want!

Top 10 Reasons Children Should Know Their Grandparents!

1. Grandparents take the time to teach their grandchildren.
2. Grandparents tell stories about their family's history.
3. Grandparents spoil their grandchildren by buying them things that parents won't.
4. Grandparents sew up those jeans that a child has torn while playing outside.
5. Grandparents have thirsty ears that eagerly listen and pay attention to their grandchildren.
6. Grandparents take grandchildren to the museum, park, arcade, or any of the fun places that kids like to visit.
7. Grandparents teach their grandchildren to pray and take them to church and Sunday School.
8. Grandparents take their grandchildren to see the doctor when their parents have to work.
9. Grandparents will stop cleaning the house, or doing their chores and start playing fun games with their grandchildren.
10. Grandparents always give the best gifts for Christmas and birthdays.

Top 10 Reasons Why Grandparents Should Know Their Grandchildren!

1. Children will be able to pass down the stories to the next generation that they learned from their grandparents.
2. Children have the face of innocence, and put a smile on their grandparent's face when there isn't much to smile about. (Grandbaby therapy)
3. Children get to learn how to bake their first batch of cookies with their grandparents.
4. Children get to share with their grandparents the first time they make an 'A' on their report card.
5. Children bring their grandparents to school to watch them in the annual school play.
6. Children get to show their grandparents' friends how smart they are by reciting verses from the Bible and participating in *The ABC Medical Terminology Spelling Bee*.
7. Children like to go outside and play, and especially like taking walks to the neighborhood store with their grandparents.
8. Children make Valentine Cards at school to hang up at their grandparents' home.
9. Children one day will grow up and become great-grandparents, because they had great grandparents.
10. Children will one day get married, and the grandparents get to pass down that invaluable family heirloom.

Grandchildren are the best source of pride, smiles and goose bumps ever invented.

Follow These Seven Steps To A Healthy Heart

Step 1: Be Spiritually Active and Reduce Negative Stress

Making faith an important part of your life can make a huge difference in your physical and emotional health. Many people who have lived to be 100 years old say that their strong religious faith is what brought them this far.

Attend a Place of Worship

Studies have shown that African Americans who attend places of worship regularly, live an average of 14 years longer than African Americans who do not. In addition to living longer, they have happier, healthier lives. While faith requires some effort, it brings rich rewards. So, find time in your life to meditate or attend a place of worship. The more spiritually active you are, the more you benefit.

From communities that provide spiritual and social support to gospel music that uplifts the soul, spirituality is an integral part of African American culture. Being spiritually active helps bring meaning to life. It encourages you to use coping strategies for life's inevitable challenges, and it provides opportunities to reach out to others. These emotional dimensions of health go hand-in-hand with your physical well-being. If, at the end of each day, you can "sit down happy" you will enjoy good health and a good life.

Use Coping Strategies

Attending a place of worship is one of several different coping strategies that can help keep stress from overpowering you. Stress is not necessarily a bad thing. In fact, experiencing stress can be good when it's manageable. Challenge can be motivating and inspiring. Stress helps wake us up in the morning, and it motivates us to take care of our responsibilities. The stress of hard work is a good thing as long as you get satisfaction from it. When stress becomes overwhelming, however, it can be destructive.

To avoid the frustration and depression that can come from destructive stress, you need tools to maintain your emotional strength and resilience. What are the best tools? Attend a place of worship. Pray. Have a positive attitude. Know your limits. Express your feelings to understanding friends and family members. Stay active in your community. Care for a child, or adopt a pet. These are important coping tools.

Reaching out to others is another important strategy for coping. When you reach out, you feel good about yourself and may help others as well. There are many ways to reach out. You might volunteer in the community, or care for a friend or family member. Maybe you listen attentively to others' concerns. You might tutor a child, help your neighbor with a home repair, or visit someone who is ill. Learn CPR and how to take an accurate blood pressure measurement so you can help others maintain their health.

You can also reach out to a pet. Studies show that people who own a pet have lower blood pressure and lower cholesterol levels than those without pets. Owning a dog might help motivate you to get out and walk often. Caring for a pet can also strengthen self-esteem and help decrease feelings of loneliness and isolation. Maybe that's why heart attack victims who have a pet survive much longer than those who don't have one.

Pursuing hobbies that you enjoy also strengthens your ability to cope. Maybe you like to garden, cook, shoot a basketball, play music, paint, play tennis or golf, or work with wood. Find time for the activities that you most enjoy and be willing to try out some new ones.

Laughter is Good Medicine

For our heart shall rejoice in Him,
because we have trusted in His holy name.
—Psalm 33:21

Actually, there is nothing wrong with either laughing or crying. They are expressions of honest human emotions that can make you feel less frustrated and less angry. Crying is a way of letting the hurt out. Even people of great faith, like King David, knew the power of lamentation. A laugh, on the other hand, is like sunshine on a cloudy day. Life without laughter is dreary. An honest laugh cheers us. It is the music, the gospel chorus of our conversations. Laughter among friends is the glue that holds people together. Victor Hugo said, "I like laughter that opens the lips and the heart, and reveals at the same time, the pearls of the soul."

In his book, *Laughter is the Best Medicine*, Dr. Norman Vincent Peale explains that certain disease ailments respond to a healthy emotional attitude, which can be prompted by laughter. A writer similarly described how he helped himself recover from cancer by watching old W.C. Fields, Bill Cosby and Flip Wilson videos.

Scientists are now discovering that laughter and a positive attitude can increase the release of endorphins and promote the manufacture of T-cells. Endorphins make us feel good and decrease our sensitivity to pain. T-cells act like sentinels in our blood to remove harmful microorganisms and cells. Chronic depression can actually weaken your immune system and lower your endorphin level. When you laugh, electrical impulses are triggered and chemicals are released into your blood stream that dull pain and tranquilize the soul. Other substances that are released with laughter improve digestion, make blood vessels relax to improve circulation, and lower blood pressure.

A philosopher said: "Laughter is the most healthful exercise. It is one of the greatest things that helps the digestion with which I am acquainted. It stirs up the blood, expands the chest, electrifies the nerves and clears away the cobwebs from the brain. It is the cheapest luxury man enjoys."

Recipe For Healthy Living

For we walk by faith, not by sight. —2 Corinthians 5:7

Here's a simple recipe to promote a healthy lifestyle. If you practice these steps you will experience the fullness and richness in life we all seek.

- 1 ounce of prevention (much better than a pound of cure)
- 5 servings of fruits and vegetables per day
- 8 glasses of water
- A dozen good friends (relatives are okay as well)
- 30 minutes of exercise per day - any kind of exercise
- 4 cups of laughter (no substitutions)
- 1 mustard seed of faith
- 2 tablespoons of patience (add more if you have children!)

Add a dash of adventure (fun can be substituted, but increase the amount). Also, add a bunch of love (enough to share). Mix well and live long.

The following ingredients are known to ruin your recipe!

- Couch potatoes
- Excessive alcohol
- Smoking
- Stress
- Negative thinking
- Negative attitude
- Excessive fats and sugar in your diet
- Complaining attitude
- Unforgiving spirit
- No social interaction

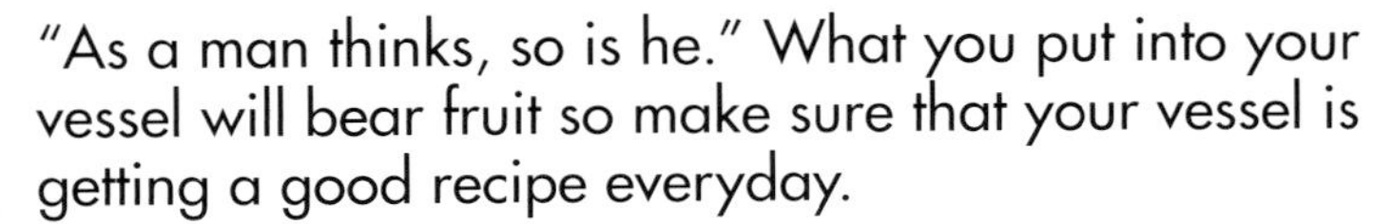

"As a man thinks, so is he." What you put into your vessel will bear fruit so make sure that your vessel is getting a good recipe everyday.

The computer people say, "Garbage in...Garbage out." Fill your life with positive experiences and the rest will take care of itself.

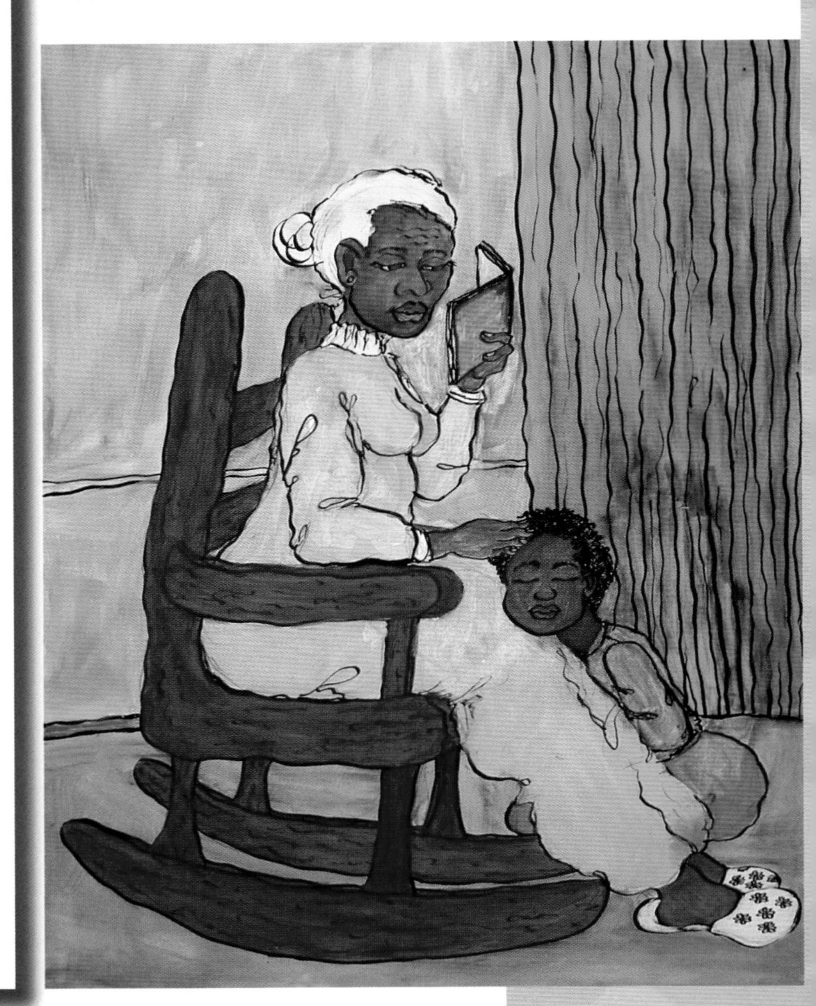

Ma Betty's Recipe to Create Loving Memories

Keke: Ma Betty, even though we are both too young to actually cook on the stove, can Woody and I help you do something?

Ma Betty: Sure you guys can help.

Woody: Learning to cook with you Ma Betty is so much fun.

Keke: What are we learning to cook today?

Ma Betty: Today, I'll show you how to make easy foods, like potatoes.

Woody: Umm… That's my favorite.

Ma Betty: Who wants to play the longest peel game?

Woody: I do.

Keke: Me too, Ma Betty

Ma Betty: Whoever's potato peel is the longest, I'll let them mash the potatoes.

Woody: Ooh, that sounds like fun!

Keke: When we get older, me and Woody will be able to cook a great meal for you, Ma Betty.

Step 2: Take Charge of Your Blood Pressure

Blood pressure is the force of blood pushing against the walls of your blood vessels. As your heart pumps blood to the cells, it creates a force in your arteries and other blood vessels. If the force is too strong or if your blood vessels are constricted, you have high blood pressure.

High blood pressure - also called hypertension - is known as the "silent killer." Most people who have it feel healthy and don't even know they have it. But if left untreated, high blood pressure can cause a heart attack, stroke, kidney failure, blindness, and even death.

African Americans are at higher risk for this serious disease than any other group. In fact, one-third of African Americans have high blood pressure! And less than one third have it under control. African Americans also tend to develop high blood pressure at a younger age than others.

Most people with high blood pressure do not have any symptoms, so the only way to know you have this disease is to have your blood pressure measured. Fortunately, this is easy to do, painless, and takes only a minute or two.

As an African American, one of the most important things you can do for your health is to get your blood pressure checked regularly. Even if you are young and feel healthy, have your blood pressure checked at least once a year. Don't be misled if you look good on the outside—it's more important to have healthy blood vessels.

If you already have high blood pressure, you should get it checked more often. Consider buying an inexpensive automatic blood pressure machine that lets you measure your blood pressure daily and provides a print-out of the results. In addition to your doctor's office or neighborhood clinic, you can get your blood pressure checked at some health clubs, shopping malls, pharmacies, or special events, such as a health fair at your church or other place of worship.

Adopting a healthy lifestyle is important for anyone with high blood pressure. But in addition to a healthy lifestyle, most people who have high blood pressure also need to take medications. Your health care provider can advise you about the many effective blood pressure medications that are available.

Measuring Blood Pressure

Your blood pressure measurement includes two numbers, such as 120/80 mm Hg. (Millimeters of mercury).

- The top, or higher number is the amount of pressure while your heart is pumping blood. This is called the systolic pressure.
- The bottom, or lower number is the amount of pressure when your heart rests between beats. This is the diastolic pressure.

A healthy blood pressure for an adult is below 135/85 mm Hg.

Even borderline blood pressure levels may increase your risk of serious health problems.

Even borderline blood pressure levels may increase your risk of serious health problems.

Remember, you can look and feel fine but still have high blood pressure. Don't wait until the damage starts before you find out you're at risk! Even children should have their blood pressure checked annually, as part of a preventive health exam.

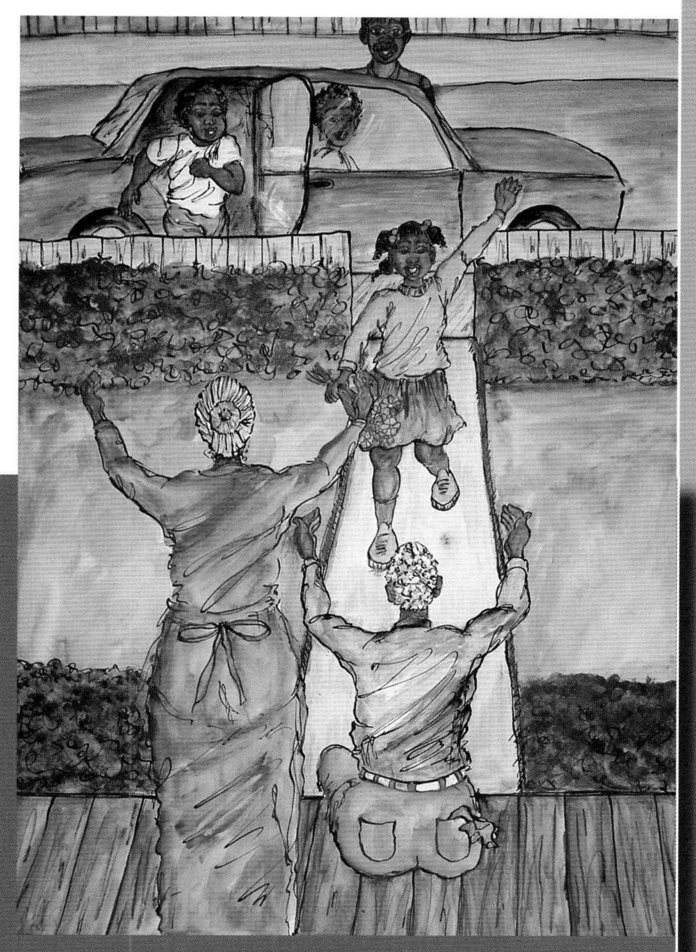

Blood Pressure Categories (for ages 18 and over)

Category	Systolic	Diastolic
Normal	Below 120	Below 80
Pre hypertensive	120-139	80-89
High blood pressure	140 or higher	90 or higher

Controlling blood pressure: Use the checklist below to examine what you are doing to help keep your blood pressure under control.

- ☐ **I get my blood pressure checked at least once a year.**
- ☐ **If my blood pressure tends to be higher than 135/85 mm Hg, I have talked with my health care provider about ways to control it.**
- ☐ **I am spiritually active.**
- ☐ **I have strategies for coping with emotional challenges.**
- ☐ **I exercise regularly.**
- ☐ **I eat foods that are low in fat and sodium.**
- ☐ **I eat plenty of fruits and vegetables.**
- ☐ **I am maintaining a healthy weight.**
- ☐ **If overweight, I am losing weight slowly.**

Step 3: Control Your Cholesterol

Do you know your cholesterol levels? You should. Monitoring your cholesterol is extremely important, because high blood cholesterol can lead to coronary heart disease, which is the leading cause of death among African Americans.

What is Coronary Heart Disease?

Your blood carries oxygen and nutrients to your heart through muscular tubes called coronary arteries. Like your kitchen sink, these arteries can become narrowed or clogged by cholesterol, calcium and fat deposits. The result is coronary heart disease.

If you have coronary heart disease, you may experience chest pain called angina when too little blood is reaching your heart. A heart attack occurs when the blood supply to part of your heart is completely blocked.

Elevated cholesterol can also lead to a stroke, which occurs when a blood vessel in the brain gets clogged or ruptures. This is a "brain attack." Other risks from clogged blood vessels include poor circulation and kidney failure.

What is Cholesterol?

Cholesterol is a waxy, fat-like substance that is naturally produced and stored in the liver. It's in the cells of your brain, muscles, skin, heart, and everywhere else that your blood flows. Your body needs cholesterol to function normally, but you only need a small amount in your bloodstream.

If you have too much blood cholesterol, your body stores extra cholesterol in your arteries, including the coronary (heart) arteries. Cholesterol build-up narrows and clogs the arteries, resulting in heart disease. The higher your cholesterol level is, the greater your risk for heart disease.

Cholesterol Tests:
What The Numbers Mean

If TOTAL cholesterol is:

Below 200	Desirable	Great! Keep below this number.
200-239	Borderline	Make changes in your lifestyle to decrease risk of a heart attack.
240 or higher	High	Danger! Seek medical help to lower your cholesterol level.

If LDL is: (Low Density Lipoprotein)

Less than 100	Optimal	Aim for low LDL.
100-129	Near optimal	
130-159	Borderline high	
160-189	Too high	
190+	Much too high	

If HDL is: (High Density Lipoprotein)

60 or higher	Optimal	Aim for high HDL
40–59	Borderline	
Less than 40	Too Low	

Good and Bad Cholesterol

There are two main types of cholesterol:

1. LDL is often called bad cholesterol, because it lays down fatty deposits in the arteries that feed your heart and brain. Too much of it puts you at risk for heart disease and stroke. Eating foods that are high in saturated fats, such as high fat meats, whole milk, cheese, and butter,

can increase your LDL, or "bad" cholesterol levels. Trans-fatty acids, found in margarine, lard, and shortening, also raise your LDL.

2. HDL is called good cholesterol, because it helps clean fat and "bad" cholesterol away from the arteries. Having a high HDL level lowers the risk of heart attack and stroke, and having a low level of HDL increases your risk. Being physically active can help raise your HDL.

Measuring Blood Cholesterol

Your health care provider can do a lipoprotein profile to measure your total cholesterol, HDL, and LDL levels. Starting at age 20, you should have this test at least every five years. Anyone with high cholesterol, diabetes, or certain other conditions should have it more often. Talk with your health care provider about how often you should have a lipoprotein profile.

If your total cholesterol or LDL levels are too high, or if your HDL level is too low, your doctor may prescribe medicine to help bring your cholesterol to a healthier level.

Controlling Cholesterol

Some of the factors that determine cholesterol levels are beyond our control. For example, your genes influence how high your LDL is by helping to determine how fast your body makes LDL and removes it from the blood. Below the age of menopause, women usually have lower cholesterol levels than men of the same age. Beginning at about age 50, cholesterol levels often rise in both men and women until they reach their early 60's.

At any age, however, following a healthy lifestyle is very important for controlling your cholesterol level. That means staying active both physically and spiritually. It means limiting the amount of fat you eat and the amount of alcohol you drink, and it means losing weight if you are overweight.

Controlling Cholesterol: Put a check mark beside the practices that you are following in your daily life. Aim to check every box.

- ☐ I am managing the stress in my life by being spiritually active and using coping strategies.
- ☐ I avoid foods that are high in saturated fat.
- ☐ I limit trans-fatty acids in my diet.
- ☐ I try not to eat foods that are high in dietary cholesterol.
- ☐ I exercise at least five days a week.
- ☐ I am not overweight (or I am succeeding in losing weight).
- ☐ I don't overindulge in alcohol.

Checking Triglycerides

The lipoprotein profile that measures your cholesterol levels will also measure your triglycerides. Triglycerides are fatty substances that your liver makes from the food you eat. People who are obese or have diabetes are likely to have high triglyceride levels. Recent studies show a strong link between high triglyceride levels and the risk of heart disease.

Triglyceride Levels (mg/dL)

Normal	Less than 150 mg/dL	Borderline risk	150-199 mg/dL
High risk	200-499 mg/dL	Very high risk	More than 500 mg/dL

If your levels are above 150 mg/dL, ask your health care provider about ways to reduce your triglycerides. In general, you need to do the same things you would do to reduce cholesterol - stick to a healthy low-fat diet and get plenty of exercise. In addition, you need to limit sugar and other carbohydrates in your diet, and if you smoke, you need to quit now! Your health care provider might also determine that you need to take medication to help control high triglyceride levels.

Harry's Big Safari

Harry: Grandpa, look! Over there behind the bushes!

Grandpa Hargrove: What do you see Harry?

Harry: A leopard and her cubs. They're so beautiful! And she's taking care of them just like you take care of me.

Grandpa Hargrove: Well, Harry, my boy, I'm glad you're enjoying the safari. And no matter what, I will always do what I can to take care of you.

Harry: Grandfather, I love you!

Grandpa Hargrove: And I love you, too!

Harry: This is *so* great!

Big Pa: Gracious Lord, as we gather to celebrate Thanksgiving, I am thankful to still have a reasonable portion of good health, for life, for my wife of 50 years, my children and grand children.

Big Ma: I am *so* thankful Dear Lord, that you have blessed this family abundantly. Continue to keep us all well, and safely nestled in the palm of your hand.

Daddy: Thank you, Heavenly Father, for blessing me with loving parents and a wonderful family.

Mommy: Lord, your grace is what gives us life each and every day. I thank you for the warm, loving family that sits around the table as we give thanks.

Tina: May the Lord's blessing touch all who are with us, especially those who prepared this meal and those who are not as fortunate to be with family on this day.

Jr.: Family is important and I appreciate you, God, for letting me be born into this great one. Bless this feast.

Big Pa: Some have meat, and no teeth. Some have teeth, and no meat. We have meat and teeth, so let's eat!

Step 4: Track Your Blood Sugar

Diabetes develops when the body has trouble producing or using insulin, causing too much sugar to build up in their blood. Having too much blood sugar (hyperglycemia) is very bad for the heart, the kidneys, and other vital organs.

Diabetes is the seventh leading cause of death in the U.S., and African Americans die from diabetes more often than whites! Furthermore, diabetes is a leading cause of heart attack, stroke, and other serious health problems, including kidney disease, impotence, blindness and amputations. Each year, more than 77,000 Americans who have diabetes die of heart disease!

There are two main types of diabetes: Type 1 and Type 2. People with Type 1 diabetes need to take insulin to say alive. Most people have Type 2. In fact, about 95% of African Americans who have diabetes have Type 2.

Regular exercise and a healthy, low-fat diet are very important for helping to prevent Type 2 diabetes. In our culture, we eat too much fatty foods and we don't get enough exercise, so more and more of us are overweight, and more and more Americans are getting diabetes.

There is no cure for diabetes. If you have diabetes, however, keeping your blood sugar level under control can be a big help in preventing heart disease and other complications. That means watching your diet, exercising, controlling your weight, and taking medication, if necessary.

Testing for Diabetes

Many people with diabetes don't even realize they have it until it becomes life-threatening or leads to a serious complication. While frequent urination and thirst should make you suspicious, the only way to find out for sure whether you have diabetes is to have a blood test. Talk with your doctor about whether you should have a diabetes blood test called a fasting plasma glucose test.

This test measures the amount of glucose, or sugar, in your blood on an empty stomach. Your doctor will ask you not to eat for at least 8 to 10 hours before the test. The results will fit into one of the four categories shown below.

Fasting Plasma Glucose Test Results (mg/dL)

Healthy	Possible risk	Impaired Glucose Tolerance	Diabetes
Below 75	75 to 110	111 to 125	126 or higher

If your test result is 126 mg/dL or higher, you probably have diabetes.

If your blood sugar is in the 111 to 125 mg/dL range, it's too high to be called healthy but too low to be called diabetes. Instead, you have a condition called impaired glucose tolerance. Like those with diabetes, people with impaired glucose tolerance are at high risk for heart attack and stroke. In fact, most people with impaired glucose tolerance eventually develop Type 2 diabetes. Recently, scientists have found that even people with blood glucose levels between 75 and 110 mg/dL may be at increased risk for heart disease, stroke, and Type 2 diabetes.

Managing Diabetes: A1C Tests

People with diabetes check their blood sugar several times a day by pricking their finger, drawing a drop of blood, and using a small glucose meter to measure the sugar level in the drop of blood.

In addition to monitoring blood sugar at home, anyone with diabetes or high glucose levels should have regular health check-ups that include a blood test called a hemoglobin A1C. If you have diabetes, expect to have the A1C test two to four times per year.

The A1C test is the best way to tell how well you are doing at controlling your glucose and insulin levels. If you get a result of less than 7, you are probably doing well. Ask your doctor what results you should expect and what they mean for you. A glucose test is equivalent to a quiz, while an AIC is equivalent to a semester test.

Prevention and Control

No matter what your blood test results, your lifestyle is the key to preventing diabetes, or managing it if you already have it.

Recently, a major study showed that if you have impaired glucose tolerance, simple changes in your diet and exercise routines can prevent diabetes. In the National Institutes of Health's Diabetes Prevention Program, exercise and weight loss reduced the risk of diabetes by nearly 60 percent among people with impaired glucose tolerance.

Why is weight control so important for preventing or controlling diabetes? Because having too much body fat makes it harder for the body to produce the insulin it needs. This is especially true if the extra fat is above the hips, rather than on the hips and thighs. This type of obesity is especially common among African American women.

Even if you aren't obese, you can get diabetes from sitting around too much, not exercising enough, and consuming a high-calorie diet. A lifestyle that adds body fat increases your risk of diabetes, which adds to your risk of heart disease.

In just the last ten years, obesity has increased by 50% and the rate of diabetes has increased 57%.

As you lose fat and build muscle, your body uses insulin better. And for most people, losing just a few pounds is enough to make a huge difference. In its Diabetes Prevention Program, the National Institutes of Health found that for most people, losing just 10 pounds is enough to cut the risk of diabetes by 58 percent!

The ABC's For Preventing Complications From Diabetes

A1C TEST. Have your blood sugar tested. If you have high blood sugar or diabetes, have an A1C test two to four times per year.

BLOOD PRESSURE. Get your blood pressure checked at least once a year

CHOLESTEROL. Have a lipoprotein profile at least once every five years, and more often if recommended by your doctor

Show A Child The Way

Granny: Robin, are you ready to go to Sunday School?

Robin: Yes, I'm ready to go Granny. Are we going to catch the bus this morning?

Granny: We sure are, Robin.

Robin: I like riding the bus to Sunday School with you Granny. This gives me a chance to have you all to myself.

Granny: I love having you all to myself too.

Robin: Do you think that we can stop and get some ice cream on the way home?

Granny: Only if you can tell me the moral of the Sunday School lesson and memorize a Bible verse.

Robin: I'll have to make sure I pay extra attention in class.

Marcus: Hey Morgan, could you pass me a drink out of the cooler?

Morgan: Only if you cut me a piece of the watermelon.

Grand Ma Jackson: This family reunion is turning out to be one of the best ever. I have all my children and grand kids here. How could this get any better?

Aunt Cheryl: You are right Momma. It can't get any better than this.

Shawn: Hey Granny, tell me who is this on the family tree?

Grand Ma Jackson: I'll tell you all about everyone on the tree after we all sit down and eat.

Greg: Mommy, where's Grand Pa Ted?

Grand Pa Ted: Here I am Greg. I'm just trying to get some more drinks out of the truck.

Grand Ma Jackson: Hey everyone, let's sit down and eat some of this good cooking.

Step 5: Enjoy Regular Exercise, Eat Smart & Manage Your Weight

If you think aging has to mean growing more sedentary or becoming disabled and useless, think again.

No matter what your age, you can continue to enjoy going out, making new friends, singing and dancing, gardening, and many other ways of staying active and having fun. Regular physical activity can help you feel better, stay healthier, and perform tasks better at any age. Why don't children jump rope anymore?

Staying physically active can lower your blood pressure and your LDL "bad" cholesterol level. It can raise your HDL "good" cholesterol level and lower your triglycerides. It helps keep blood sugar under control to prevent the serious complications of diabetes. Exercise is also crucial if you need to lose weight, and it's a wonderful way to help keep stress from overpowering you.

Every little bit of exercise helps a little bit. So, resist the temptation to take the escalator instead of the stairs, or to park right next to your doorway. Resist the temptation to ride in a wheel chair if you can manage without it. You don't have to let society and people who mean well, turn you into an invalid!

Exercise Daily

To help make regular exercise a lifelong habit, consider exercising with a family member or a friend. You might like to talk with your friends while walking around the neighborhood. Maybe you could start an exercise group at your place of worship. Or maybe you can walk a dog. Even if you don't have an exercise partner, there are a lot of ways to make physical activity a part of your everyday life. Whenever you have the opportunity...

DANCE! DANCE! DANCE!

Consider Adding Some of These Activities to Your Daily Routine.

Put a check mark beside the activities that appeal to you.

- ☐ Get off the bus one or two stops early so that you end up walking farther.
- ☐ Park at the far end of the parking lot, or park a few blocks away from your destination and walk.
- ☐ Ministers can set a good example by giving up those prized parking spaces.
- ☐ Use the stairs instead of the elevator.
- ☐ Get up 15 minutes earlier in the morning and stretch.
- ☐ Work out along with an exercise video.
- ☐ Play your favorite dance music. Do the steps you know and enjoy, and add some new moves.
- ☐ Play tag or other active games with your grandchildren
- ☐ Ride a stationary bike while watching TV.
- ☐ Keep a pair of walking shoes at your office, and take walks during lunch or breaks, either on your own or with a co-worker.

Follow An Exercise Plan

No matter what your age, try to be active for at least 30 minute a day. You can do activities by yourself or with others. You can d 30 minutes all at once, or you can exercise two or three times a day for 10-15 minutes at a time. If you have a health problem, b sure to talk to your doctor before starting an exercise program.

The key to a successful exercise program is to find the activitie that you enjoy doing and that fit into your daily routine. Which o the following activities would you like to include in your plan?

MODERATE ACTIVITIES

Walking
Gardening
Dancing
Vacuuming
Raking leaves
Climbing stairs
Yoga
Bowling
Golf

VIGOROUS ACTIVITIES

Bicycling
Jogging or running
Walking at a brisk pace
Aerobics
Swimming or water aerobics
Basketball
Soccer or Football
Baseball
Tennis

If you aren't used to exercising, start with moderate activities and work your way up.

You may decide simply to walk 30 minutes each day. Or, you might prefer a combination of activities. For example, you might attend a fitness class one day a week, vacuum the house on another day, go out dancing on weekends, and take walks or climb stairs on the other days.

Eat Smart

A traditional "healthy" breakfast used to be eggs, bacon, sausage, pancakes, hash browns, doughnuts and buttered biscuits. But now we know that a bowl of whole grain cereal with a sliced banana and skim milk is a much more healthy breakfast. In fact, there are many delicious options. Try fresh blueberries on almond granola with skim milk or with yogurt. Be creative— it's fun and it's healthier. Eating smart means eating foods that are low in fat and rich in nutrients. It means eating lots of fruits, vegetables, and whole grains. And most importantly, drink pure, clean, cold refreshing water instead of sugar water in the form of sodas, Kool-Aid and sweet tea.

Eating right isn't just about living longer. It's about feeling good. It's about staying healthy and vigorous even as you age. Smart eating helps you avoid having a heart attack, stroke, high blood pressure, or diabetes. It helps to prevent suffering and increase the healthy years that lie ahead.

Eating smart also means not eating too much. It means having the strength to resist people who push the food they've prepared for you. Beware of food pushers. Don't let anyone make you feel guilty about limiting how much you eat! And don't feel compelled to eat what the kids leave on the table. It's better to throw away food than to eat extra stuff that you don't need.

Cut Fat and Cholesterol

Eating too much saturated fat can clog your arteries and lead to a heart attack, diabetes or stroke. Saturated fat raises your "bad" cholesterol levels more than other types of fat. To reduce saturated fat in your diet, eat less butter, cheese, whole milk, lard, and fatty cuts of meat.

Trans-fatty Acids may also raise your bad cholesterol levels. To reduce trans-fatty acids in your diet, eat less margarine, shortening, and snacks or desserts that contain hydrogenated vegetable oil. Ask a nutrition advisor about healthy alternatives to butter and margarines like Benecol.

Dietary Cholesterol is in foods that come from animals. Meats, poultry, and dairy products contain high levels of dietary cholesterol in addition to saturated fat. Foods that are especially high in dietary cholesterol include egg yolks and organ meats, such as liver and kidney. There is no cholesterol in foods that come from plants, including fruits, vegetables and grains.

Monounsaturated Fats and **Polyunsaturated Fats** are preferred and may lower LDL cholesterol. Canola, olive, and peanut oils are high in monounsaturated fat. Sesame and sunflower oils are high in polyunsaturated fat.

Food labels show the amount of various types of fat in each serving as a percentage of total daily calories. Limit polyunsaturated fat to 10 percent of your total daily calories. Another 10 to 15 percent of total calories can come from monounsaturated fat.

Enjoy Fruits and Vegetables

The easiest way to cut fat and cholesterol is to fill up on your favorite fruits and vegetables. Also try to eat whole grains, such as whole wheat bread, oatmeal, and whole grain cereals. Beans are also healthy and a good source of protein. Dr. Keith Ferdinand's father use to say: "The meat is in the beans."

Try to eat at least five servings per day of fruits and vegetables. If you've ever gone on a "diet," you know that it's not easy to change how you eat. You may need support from friends or family members in your effort to change. You can also get support from your doctor.

To help keep your blood pressure down:

Eat less sodium. Food labels tell how much sodium is in a product. Instead of using convenience foods that are high in sodium, prepare your own meals from scratch. Try not to cook with much salt. Instead, use spices, herbs, and salt-free seasoning blends. Spice things up with a dash of Mrs. Dash, a salt substitute.

Golf: The Metaphor for Life

Ricky: Keep on going baby. It looks like its going in Pa Pa Joe. Yeah, that's it, right in the hole.

Pa Pa Joe: Great shot! You made that putt look easy.

Ricky: I'm getting pretty good like Pa Pa Joe.

Pa Pa Joe: You surely are, Ricky. If you keep playing like this, you may be the next Tiger Woods!

Ricky: I'm not that good yet. I'm just learning.

Pa Pa Joe: If you keep coming out to the links with your Pa Pa Joe, who knows how good you could be.

Ricky: Do you really believe I have what it takes?

Pa Pa Joe: Well Ricky, everything has a starting, middle, and an end point. If you follow through from the beginning to the end, you are destined for success.

Ricky: I'm glad that you have so much confidence in me. It's good to know I'll always have you in my corner.

Pa Pa Joe: Come on "Tiger." Lets go to the next hole.

Manage Your Weight

You're not alone if you are carrying around extra pounds. Unfortunately, nearly 2 out of 3 adults in the United States are overweight or obese, according to the Surgeon General's latest report. The rates are even higher among African American women.

Don't be misled by magazines that promote being large as attractive. Obesity is not a beauty issue. It's a health issue. The most important reason to lose weight is that you'll feel better and stay healthier. Having extra body fat can lead to a heart attack, stroke, diabetes and other serious health problems. Losing even just a small amount of weight is likely to help in several ways:

- Lowering your blood pressure (thus decreasing your risk of heart attack and stroke).
- Eliminating LDL "bad" cholesterol and triglycerides (thus decreasing your risk of cardiovascular disease).
- Keeping your blood sugar from rising (thus decreasing your risk of diabetes).
- Increasing self-esteem.
- Decreasing depression.
- Reducing your risk of arthritis.

Your genes, your environment, and emotional factors can all contribute to obesity. No matter what the causes are, it boils down to this: You are taking in more calories than you use. In other words, your energy balance is lopsided.

If you've ever tried to lose weight, you know how hard it is to keep the pounds off and not regain the weight you've lost. Plenty of diets and pills promise a quick and easy way to shed pounds, but there aren't really any shortcuts or magic ways to lose weight and keep it off. Stick to the basics: set reasonable weight-loss goals; get plenty of exercise; and eat less.

Set Your Weight Goal

Your first step toward losing weight should be to talk with a doctor, dietitian, or nutritionist to help set a realistic weight goal. To reach your goal safely, aim to lose no more than five pounds per week.

After you achieve your first goal, you can set a new goal. If you are 30 pounds overweight, for example, you might try to lose 10 pounds in the next two months, then set a goal to lose another 10 pounds.

Stay Active

Find ways everyday to be physically active. You will also find it easier to lose weight if you stay spiritually active and keep stress from overwhelming you.

Cut Calories

To lose weight, try to eat about 300 calories less than usual each day (About 2 cans of soda). Calorie consumption also depends on how active you are. We can all do well by consuming less than 2,000 calories per day.

How to cut Calories:

1. Choose foods that are lower in fat and calories.
2. Reduce or eliminate foods that have calories but not nutrients. That means you should eat less fat and sugar and drink less alcohol.
3. Enjoy fruits, vegetables, and whole grains - foods that have lots of nutrients and roughage. Eat fruits rather than drink fruit juices especially artificially flavored and concentrated juices.
4. Eat foods that are high in fiber. Fiber is useful for weight control because eating enough of it can help you feel full and not eat too much.
5. Eat smaller portions. Exercising or drinking a glass of water before a meal can help reduce your appetite.
6. Stick to a well-rounded diet.
7. Study the nutrition facts on food labels.

Grandparents Rule!!!

Kenya: We've always been told that Christmas is not only a time of caring and sharing, but a time to reflect on the birth of our Lord and Savior, Jesus Christ.

Kevin: When Kenya and I come to Grams and Gramps' house for the holiday, they always have us give thanks for *"love, life and the people who love us."* Is that your favorite prayer, Gramps?

Grams: That's the spirit of the season, my darlings! It's love, not gifts that is the most important thing.

Gramps: While Jesus is the reason for Christmas, Grams and I love you both very much. From the bottom of our hearts, we have several gifts for you too. Merry Christmas!

Going For The Fence

Chauncy: I'm going to knock it over the fence like Barry Bonds.

Grand Pa Taylor: Are you ready for the heat, Chauncy?

Chauncy: Come on Grand Pa Taylor, toss it up here.

Grand Pa Taylor: Here it comes. BAM!!!

Chauncy: Look at it! It's going, going, gone!

Grand Pa Taylor: Yep, there it goes. What a hit!

Chauncy: I told you I could do it.

Grand Pa Taylor: You sure did, Chauncy. We are going to have to sign you up for summer league ball this year.

The Gift of Music

Timmy: Will you teach me how to play your guitar, Papi?

Papi: Sure, Timmy! Playing the guitar is my favorite passion, next to spending time with you.

Timmy: Really Papi? Teaching me seems to be just as much fun for you, as it is for me.

Papi: It gives me the chance to teach you something fun, along with teaching you other things.
Timmy: When I'm older, and still playing your guitar, I'll always remember what you taught me.
Papi: If you learn to play the guitar, you can have it when you get older.

The Average American's Annual Intake of Junk Food

The average annual intake of low nutrient-density foods in the U.S. consists of:

756 doughnuts
60 pounds of cakes & cookies
23 gallons of ice cream
7 pounds of potato chips
22 pounds of candy
200 sticks of gum
365 servings of soda pop
90 pounds of fat
134 pounds of refined sugar

Source: Dr. William Richardson, Atlanta, GA

We've Got To Do Better Than This!

"NO" FOODS*	"YES" FOODS
Bacon Sugar	Oatmeal or other whole grain cereals
Cakes, Buns & Pasteries	Greens
Sausage	Whole wheat bread
Egg yolks	Rye bread
Hash browns	Baked potato
French fries	Sweet potato or yams
All Fried foods	Grilled or baked foods
Cheeseburgers	Yogurt
Hot dogs	Fish
Potato chips	Turkey (skinless)
Doughnuts	Chicken (skinless)
Salami/bologna	Garlic, onions
Pizza	Salad
Whole milk	Carrots, broccoli, vegetables
Cream	Apples, bananas, fruits
Butter	Skim milk
Candy	Fruits
Soft Drinks	Water

* These should NEVER touch your lips. Every little bit hurts a little bit.

Step 6 Don't Smoke

More than 390,000 people die each year from cigarette smoking due to lung cancer and premature death from heart diseases. Smoking also causes chronic bronchitis and emphysema. Reports have shown that persons who have stopped smoking for five years, their lungs heal and look almost brand new, just as if they had never smoked. The Surgeon General of the United States warns that cigarette smoking is harmful to your health and can cause death. In addition, smoking during pregnancy may cause damage to an unborn baby.

Passive smoking (inhaling someone else's smoke), causes 5,000 lung cancer and heart disease deaths each year. Not the least of the reasons to stop smoking are: it makes your clothing and hair smell badly; wrinkles your skin; wastes money; stains your teeth; makes food tasteless; and gives you an annoying cough. Smoking stinks!

If you smoke and want to stop, use the following tips to help you:

1. Set a date to quit.
2. Inform friends, family, and coworkers of your plan to quit and ask for their support.
3. Throw away cigarettes, matches, and lighters in your home and car.
4. Review previous attempts to quit. Try to assess why they failed, and what you can do to avoid those obstacles.
5. Anticipate challenges and plan what to do instead of smoking.
6. Keep busy and have a supply of low calorie snacks on hand.

Step 7 Access Better Healthcare

"I will give you the keys of the kingdom of heaven, and whatever you bind on earth will be bound in heaven, and whatever you loose on earth will be loosed in heaven."

Matthew 16:19

Despite the fact that the life expectancy of African Americans has increased by 100% over the last 100 years and steady continuous improvement in the overall health of the U.S. population, racial and ethnic minorities experience higher rates of serious illness and death than whites. African Americans, for example, experience the highest rates of heart disease, cancer, strokes and HIV/AIDS than any other groups. The reasons for these health disparities are complex and poorly understood, but may reflect differences in socioeconomic status, health related risk factors, and environmental degradation, as well as direct and indirect consequences of discrimination.

Common Barriers to Equal Access to Health Care

- Lack of healthcare insurance - Lack of health coverage has consequences for uninsured individuals, the health care system, and society as a whole. The uninsured are more likely to encounter difficulty obtaining care and use fewer health care services. Many of the uninsured go without needed primary and preventive care that may avert a serious health crisis.

- Geographic — The location of the healthcare provider is often a barrier. In urban settings, a person may have to take two buses and the subway to get to their doctor. People living in rural communities may have to travel several miles to a larger town to get appropriate care.

- Language and culture — Effective communication can be difficult if the language and/or culture of the patient and the healthcare provider are different.

- Low Health Literacy — Understanding medical terminology can be intimidating for some people. Take the time to read educational brochures that you run across. They will help increase your health literacy, and guide you in understanding which questions to ask. It is important to become an active partner with your doctor. Ask questions until you get satisfactory answers. Remember, the best doctors are only human, so the more you understand your own condition, the better equipped you will be to help manage it.

Some people are fearful of doctors and healthcare establishments. This fear stems from the re-telling of stories about negative experiences (real and imagined) of other people. You should not assume that your experiences will mirror those of your parents or grandparents. You should not ignore health problems no matter how big or small. Denial will not make a problem go away. It is very important that you keep track of your health status. You must resist the temptation to believe that what you don't know can't hurt you.

Take advantage of any medical benefits provided by your employer. Everyone, no matter how healthy, should see a physician every 1-3 years depending upon age and medical history, this will allow you to identify problems early, and have more options for treatment. A clean bill of health at age 40 does not automatically mean that it will be clean at age 50. You must check in periodically with a healthcare provider to know for sure.

"Disparities in the healthcare delivered to racial and ethnic minorities are real and are associated with worse outcomes in many cases, which are unacceptable. The real challenge lies not in debating whether disparities exist, because the evidence is overwhelming. But in developing and implementing strategies to reduce and eliminate them."

--Alan Nelson, M.D., former president of the American Medical Association and chair of the committee that wrote the Institute of Medicine report, "Unequal Treatment: Confronting Racial and Disparities in Health Care."

"Longevity has its virtue. Of all the forms of inequality, injustice in health is the most shocking and inhumane."

(Dr. Martin Luther King, Jr. - 1966)

ENJOY YOUR PROGRESS

Congratulations! By reading this book you have taken a giant step toward a healthier heart.

Don't be discouraged if you are finding that you need to make a lot of changes in your lifestyle. Nobody expects you to make all of these changes overnight. But remember, every little bit helps. Every step you take in the right direction will make it that much easier to take the next step.

It was Eubie Blake who said, "If I'd have known I was going to live this long, I would have taken better care of myself." This is an excellent reason for you to start taking better care of yourself, starting today! If you don't already have a health care provider whom you see regularly, it's time to find one. You need someone with whom you feel comfortable. Think of it as a partnership: You and your doctor are working on a project, and the project is your health. Before each visit, write down a list of the questions you have. Then, make sure you get answers to all your questions. It may be helpful to bring a friend along. If there isn't time to get all the answers you need, talk with your doctor about this. If he or she isn't responsive, it may be time to find a different doctor.

It is our hope that the health messages combined with the beautiful illustrations and vignettes will inspire you to change unhealthy behaviors so that you are around to help your children and their children and their children's children to become healthy, happy, well adjusted adults. Let's begin this journey.

You're not just doing this for yourself. You're taking care of yourself for your family, your grandchildren, and for all of your loved ones. Take pride in your accomplishments. You deserve it!

As The Praises Go Up, The Blessings Come Down

Poo Bear: Granny, Granny. Are you ready to come tuck us into bed?

Granny: Yes, Poo Bear. But, first don't forget what you guys have to do before bedtime.

Jeana: Oh yeah, how could we forget to say our prayers.
"Now I lay down to sleep, I pray the Lord my soul to keep...."

Poo Bear: Did you learn to pray when you were our age Granny?

Granny: I sure did. Great leaders like Martin Luther King, Jr. taught that a family that prays together, stays together.

A Helping Hand

G-Pop: If you don't tie your shoes right,the laces will trip you, Roscoe.

Roscoe: I know, G-Pop. You tell me that every time we go outside to play ball. Can you help me? You tie my shoes tighter than I do, and I like when you do it.

G-Pop: Sure, Roscoe! I'll do it this one last time, just for you.

Roscoe: Thanks, G-Pop! Until the next time.

Staying Young At Heart

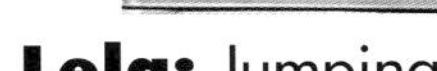

Lela: Jumping rope is fun, Grandma and Grandpa. Can we do this all the time?

Grandma: Baby, we can do this as often as you like. It gets your Grandpa out of that chair and into the yard for some fresh air and a tiny bit of exercise.

Michael: Grandpa gets lots of exercise because I keep him going, just for fun.

Grandpa: That's right! The next time you two come over, Grandma and I will do some jumping.

Grandma: Babies, you two remember who said that... and be sure to hold him to it. Grandma will be watching!

Suga: Wow Grand Pa. Look over there!

Grand Pa: Those are the Ancient Pyramids of Egypt. Those Great Pyramids are over 4,000 years old.

Grand Ma: Now, that's even older than your Grand Pa!

Grand Pa: Suga, those Pyramids were built by the Ancient Egyptians.

Suga: Who were the Ancient Egyptians?

Grand Ma: They were a great civilization that once ruled the known world. Some of the richest and most powerful people in history lived during that period.

Grand Pa: It sometimes took over 10 years to build just one Pyramid!

Suga: 1, 2, 3, 4, 5, 6, 7, 8, 9, 10. I'm only 7, so that's even older than me Grand Pa.

Grand Ma: Could you imagine the amount of walking they did?

Grand Pa: We know they didn't have to worry about not getting enough exercise.

Suga: This has been the best vacation ever. Where are we going next?

We are An Ancient People

Grandparent's Story:

Mr. Rondereo Sidney

I grew up in Meridian, Mississippi where I had the gift of love and comfort from the matriarch of our family, my grandmother, Birtie Sidney. "Big Momma" as we call her, was my second mother, so to speak.... She was the pride of our family as well as her church and the community... Savoy, where she lived. She'd tell you in a minute that the "doors flew back on welcome hinges" at our church, New Prospect Missionary Baptist Church. She is always imparting fond remembrances of our family, or uttering prayers of thanksgiving for how we've grown. Just to hear her witness how thankful she is to have raised twelve children and live as long as she has makes her all the more special.

She taught us the importance of respect for others, especially our elders. She always has a genuine word of encouragement to impart. It's her gift of making everyone feel important and better because they met her. My Grandmother always took the time to answer our questions and to let us know how proud she was of us.

Big Momma is part of a community that values its children. It was a joy to visit her because she always kept some goodies or could bake up a surprise in no time. She was a great cook! At the dinner table, you were guaranteed to hear what foods were good for you. She encouraged us to eat our vegetables, even if we didn't like them. And most of the time we were obedient because we knew she'd be proud of us, if we did. We had cousins that lived in her neighborhood and friends that made for fun times around her house. Big Momma helped us realize that what we did and how we lived mattered. It mattered not only to her and the family but to the whole community.

The seeds of awareness were planted in those early years of my childhood by "Big Momma." Awareness of who I was. Awareness that I was a small but valuable part of a whole. Awareness that what I did had consequences, not only for me, but my entire family.

Grandparent's Story:

Ms. LaTrese Coyt

My grandmother, Eva Woodruff, is still able and feisty at age 81. She's still a fashion conscious diva with grace and charm who allowed her oldest granddaughter to raid her closet for clothes, when I could fit them. That's just a part of the bonding that we've shared. She's been in my life forever, and in my children's lives today, which is a blessing.

Church was a natural part of my life growing up. My mother and grandmother instilled in me early on, the importance of being grounded in faith. I was known as "Eva's grandbaby" at her church, Antioch Missionary Baptist, where she served for many years as a nurse. My female relatives were all very protective of me. My independence and strong resolve are inherited character traits from these wonderful women.

I am fortunate to have had another grandmother to share a close relationship with. Her name was Othella Gibson, my stepfather's mother who is now deceased. She came into my life at an early age with a beautiful spirit of love and caring that made her my magnet.

As a child, I could always go to her house and she 'd make me peanut brittle and I could eat as much as I wanted. Whenever I wanted some attention or wasn't feeling well, she'd put me in her lap, cover me with a blanket and rub my stomach. She was a constant shower of affection. All the women of my life helped to shape my personality and transferred to me a determined spirit with the sense of caring and compassion that I have today.

Personal
Grandparent and Grandchildren Photographs
go here.

Grandparents Are Libraries-- Check-out A Book Regularly

Grand Dad: Hey Pumpkin, would you like to read your ole Grand Dad one of your books?

Pumpkin: Sure Grand Dad. Let's read my favorite book, *"Go Run, Go Play."* You know why this is my favorite book?

Grand Dad: Why Pumpkin?

Pumpkin: Grand Dad, you don't remember? This is the first book that you taught me how to read when I was just 4 years old. Now that I'm a big girl, I can read it all on my own.

Grand Dad: I'm happy that I was able to teach you how to read. During your Great Grand Dad's time, when he was a slave, we were not allowed to read.

Pumpkin: Why Grand Dad?

Grand Dad: It's hard to control people with nonsense when they are educated. To read was thought of as a privilege.

Pumpkin: I'm sure glad that I have the privilege to read. It is so much fun, especially when we do it together.

How Do I Love You-- Let Me Count The Ways

Gramps: Since the weather is bad outside, lets stay inside and find something to do.

Doody: What will we do?

Gramps: Doody, why don't we learn some math, then we will play your favorite game.

Doody: Riding on your back and playing horsy is my favorite play time game.

Gramps: Then that settles it; that's what we will play. First, you have to show me what you learned in math class this week.

Doody: We learned our 9's multiplication table. "9; 18; 27; 36; 45; 54; 63; 72; 81; 90."

Gramps: That's just Great Doody. Keep up the good work. If you keep learning at this pace, who knows. My granddaughter may become a great scientist or doctor some day.

Doody: Can we play now?

Gramps: Sure Doody, you've earned it.

9
18
27
36
45
54
63
72
81
90
99
108

Afternoon Safari

Allen: Granny, Oscar and I like coming to the zoo.

Oscar: Yeah Granny, me and Allen love coming to the zoo with you and learning about the different types of animals.

Granny: I love coming with you too. Do you know what type of animals those are?

Allen: They are called elephants, right?

Granny: Yes, that is correct Allen. Did you know that there are two species of elephants; the African and Asian elephant.

Oscar: What kind of elephants are those?

Granny: Lets read the description on the sign.

Allen: "These animals are African elephants which roam the Southern region of Africa. Besides the whales of the ocean, elephants are the largest mammals on Earth!

Oscar: Whoa, that's big Granny! I wonder what's at the next stop?

Allen: Lets go see.

Grandma's Grandma's Quilt

Neicey: Ah Big Momma, it's beautiful!

Big Momma: Well Neicey, it's time to pass it along to you.

Neicey: Is it really mine? I can't believe it!

Big Momma: We have passed this quilt down from generation to generation since before the Civil War. And now, it's your time.

Neicey: This is just the greatest gift that anyone has ever given me.

Big Momma: You just make sure that you pass this family heir loom along to your grandchild and that they know it's importance to our family.

Neicey: I know growing up as a kid, I always dreamed that I would one day own it. Now, just like my wedding, that day is finally here.

Big Momma: Well, tomorrow will be your turn to carry on a great tradition and to "Jump the Broom."

Lessons of Life

Zoo Keeper: Hi guys, welcome to the Zoo Aroma's Reptile Area. My name is Denise Brown.

Jeremy: Hey, Ms. Brown, what kind of snake is that?

Zoo Keeper: Boys and Girls, this reptile is called a Boa constrictor. Some snakes can be harmful, but not this one.

Alexis: Where do these type of snakes come from?

Zoo Keeper: Boas can be found from Northern Mexico all the way down to Argentina.

Sly: Where did this one come from?

Zoo Keeper: This one was found in the Belize rainforest.

Denardo: How big do they get?

Zoo Keeper: They can grow to be 10 feet long, and weigh over 60 pounds.

Jeremy: Can we touch it?

Zoo Keeper: Sure, but be careful. We don't want to hurt it.

A Grandparent's Story
B. Waine Kong, Ph.D, JD

After my father abandoned us, my mother took us to live with her mother, so she could accept a job in the United States. Her monthly checks and care packages supported us along with our extended family. (Our house was so small, we had to go outside to change our minds!). I was four years old and my brother, Earl, was three. Grandmother lived in a little farming village on the countryside called Woodlands, in St. Elizabeth's Parish, Jamaica. Her name was Rosella "Rosie" McKenzie. It was a quaint, tropical, rural setting with no modern conveniences. These were proud, hard working people whose annual household income is still less than $500.00 per year. My brother and I were nurtured by a quiet, assuring grandmother whose love and affection abounded. She was a godly woman who kept us entertained with stories about her youth as well as from the Bible. Granny had a beautiful peace about her that made us always feel secure and loved as she sang hymns from the moment she said "good morning" to the moment she said "good night."

I recall endearing moments of her sitting in her rocker telling us stories or reading to us. My favorite place was right on the floor in front of her, within reach of her hand that lovingly stroked my hair. I often think of those moments when I'm with my own children and grandchildren. I lived with her for about 10 years while attending the Springfield All Ages School until age fifteen. Granny and I had a special bond. She was extremely proud of my achievements. I felt honored that it pleased her that I was a fast learner. I was appointed "man of the house," and entrusted with chores and responsibilities that aided my quest for learning. She taught me to care for the crops and farm animals, pick vegetables and fruits, and manage the household budget. I learned about leadership and Christian values from this marvelous woman who was always attentive to my curiosity.

Our Sunday routine was waking up to Granny's singing and praying as she prepared our breakfast of hot milk, hard dough bread and butter, ackee and salt fish. It was our favorite day of the week. We walked the two miles to church together, greeting friends and neighbors we rarely saw during the week. Sunday service was a spirited message of salvation.

We had a very entertaining "teaching moment" in the form of our own little 'Ted Mack's Amateur Hour' at home each Sunday afternoon. We'd return home to a special feast of brown-stew chicken, rice and peas, and sweet potato pudding. After dinner, we'd clear off the table, that became our stage as I pretended to be the preacher. I would re-enact as much of his message as I could, to include hand gestures and expressions. Granny would provide suggestions (between laughs) that helped us recite Bible passages correctly. Sunday evening, we'd visit relatives and friends. This was a wonderful form of family entertainment. From these episodes, I became confident enough to be an actor in plays at church and at school. Granny taught us about character and the importance of being respectful and truthful. "Your reputation is everything..." she would say.

She told us many humorous stories of her youth, and about her husband, who died before I was born. In later years, I realized that the women in my family were outliving the men. I have six aunts who have all outlived their husbands. I jokingly call them "the Black widows."

Today, I have three lovely grandchildren who keep me busy thinking of ways to surprise them like the time I prepared a special treasure chest and hunt for them. I made a treasure of all of the coins that I'd collected over five years and placed them along with beads and memorabilia, stuffed in a treasure chest. I sketched out a map, crumbled the paper and burned the edges to give it an antiqued look. Then, I placed it where my grand kids could discover it. As you could imagine, the treasure hunt began. We followed the map together, making certain to visit each step of the journey until we discovered the spot! The children were really excited to reach the point of the buried treasure.

I dug up the chest I'd buried the day before. They uncovered a bounty of more than one hundred dollars in coins, plus beads and trinkets to share. They spent the rest of the day dividing it up.

We visit each other often and we make it a point to take them on special trips, particularly to Jamaica, to taste a little of their heritage.

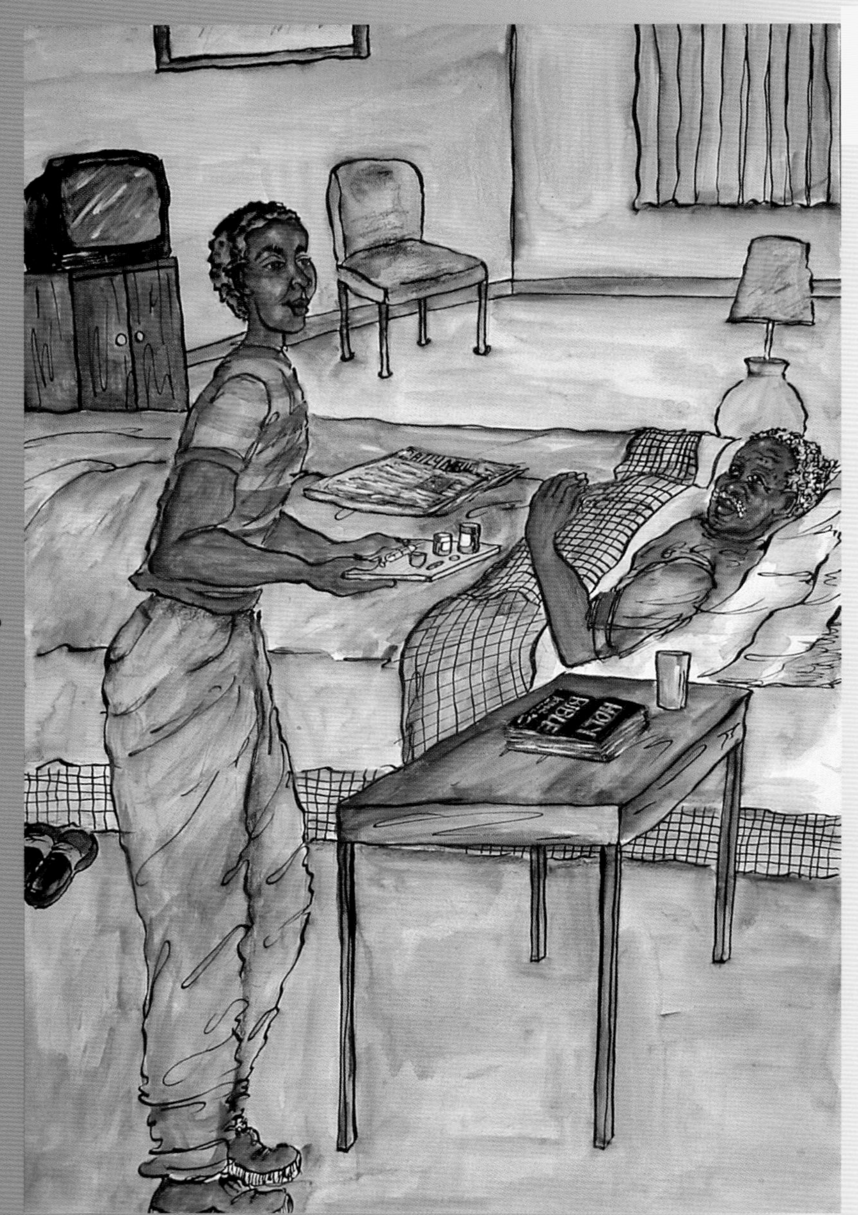

Lean On Me, When You're Not Strong

Charles: Hey, Grand Pa Curry. Are you ready to get your medication and insulin shot?

Grand Pa Curry: I'm ready as I'm going to be.

Charles: Which one do you want to take first?

Grand Pa Curry: Let's take that one there, Charles. I have the hardest time swallowing those big pills.

Charles: O.K. Let's take the blue one first.

Grand Pa Curry: Now let's take that one. Charles, I'll need you to inject my insulin shot for me, my boy. I'm feeling a little too weak to do it myself today.

Charles: No problem, Grand Pa. Be nice and still now; I don't want to stick you too hard.

Grand Pa Curry: Thanks, Charles. That didn't hurt at all. You'd better make sure you eat right and continue to exercise, that way you won't have to be like me and take these insulin shots.

Charles: I'll make sure to do that, Grand Pa. I think I'd like to become a doctor. That way, I can really take care of people like you.

The "Hook Up"

Tesha: Hi Big Momma. How you doing?

Big Momma: I'm doing good, Baby.

Tesha: I received the "goody" box that you sent me. Thank you so very much!

Big Momma: You know I'm always thinking about my grand child. Somebody has to look out for my baby while she is off to college.

Tesha: You know what, Big Momma?

Big Momma: What is it, Baby?

Tesha: I was not expecting this at all. How did you know that I needed everything that you sent?

Big Momma: You know, that is what Grannies are for, to make sure that their grand kids are taken care of.

Tesha: They surely do. Thanks much! Big Momma, you're the best!

Big Momma: By the way, how is everything going at school?

Tesha: Things just got a whole lot better with this box full of "goodies" you sent! I love you, Big Momma.

Making Practice Perfect

Sonny: Gramps, would you like to play catch with me and Spot in the backyard?

Gramps: OK Sonny, let's go out back and toss the ball a while.

Sonny: Come on Spot, lets go in the backyard.

Sonny: When I play kick-ball with my friends in the neighborhood, everyone always wants me on their team. They tell me that I'm the best catcher in the neighborhood. Look at Spot trying to catch his ball Gramps!

Gramps: He sure looks like he is having as much fun as we are.

Sonny: He surely does.

Sonny: Who would have ever thought that playing catch with you in the backyard all those years would pay off?

Gramps: Like I always told you, "Practice makes perfect." So remember Sonny, whatever you do in this world, practice, practice, practice, and be the best you can be.

The Mediator and The Advocate... Everybody Needs One

Grand Dad: Mama. Boys will be boys. Stop all that fussin!

Mama: He needs to do his work, when I tell him to!

Grand Dad: He'll do what you asked him to do, right Scooter?

Scooter: Yes, Sir. I'll get on it right away, Mama. (Thank God for Grand Dad. He helps me out when I get in trouble with Mama.) My work will be done in a flash!

Grandparents and grandchildren get along because they have a common enemy.

A Grandparent's Story: Paul Underwood, M.D.

Grandparents are very important to us in many ways, especially in tying the family together historically. That's because they know where they came from, they can see where the family is presently, and that's because they know from whence they came. Thanks to their grandchildren, they can best relate to the promises of the future. Grandparents are our best advocates for celebrating the culture and communicating family traditions. Grandparents keep our ancestral link alive by identifying qualities and similarities in character traits among the fore parents and other relatives.

When children get unruly, as parents, we are driven sometimes to raising our voices, chasing them around or resorting to a more physical means of control. Grandparents, on the other hand, possess a gift of controlling children that the parents often do not have. It probably stems from the respect and awe the grandchild has for their Mom or Dad's mother or father. The grandparents have it! They can get an immediate and obedient response to their requests, with just a look or a single motion of the hand. My grandmother just looks them in the eye and claps her hands twice, and my kids stop whatever negative behavior they're up to. It's great! When I ask her how she was able to do that, she replies, "It's just one of the secrets of being a grandparent."

I grew up in the company of grandmother and my great-grandmother on my father's side. They were Maggie Guyton and Louise Underwood. My great grandmother played the guitar. It fascinated me as child that my grandmother had such a unique and interesting talent. The fact that she played encouraged me to begin to play the bass guitar about 10 years later. We, as it turned out, were the only family members with an inclination to play such an instrument.

On my mother's side, I had my grandfather and his wife, Ralph and Anna Lou. All the time I knew her, she suffered from multiple sclerosis. Her nickname was "Kit" because she purred like a kitten. In retrospect, this may have been one of the earliest signs of her condition.

Grandpa Martin cared for her with a calm, committed spirit, until she developed recurrent pulmonary edema. In later years, I remember a few episodes of having to rush her to the hospital when she suffered from attacks of heart failure, and couldn't breathe. Today, as a heart specialist, I can readily identify with what families are experiencing when they bring family members into the hospital in that state. Unfortunately, from my great-grandmother Louise, I was taught the meaning of sudden cardiac death. This grandmother suffered from advanced multiple sclerosis. She was found in a chair with a bottle of Malox in her hand.

Grandparents provide insight into a family's health history. They keep us abreast of common medical conditions that run in the family. They can best bind together what kinds of health related problems are common among family members. This kind of information can help all of us make amends to our own health. Grandparents are an invaluable source of insight into the family; the personality traits, the common health conditions, and bear true witness to living a healthy life.

Heart Fact:
The normal heart is a strong, muscular pump a little larger than a fist. It pumps blood continuously through the circulatory system. Each day the average heart "beats" (expands and contracts) 100,000 times and pumps about 2,000 gallons of blood. In a 70-year lifetime, an average human heart beats more than 2.5 billion times.

A Bundle of Joy

Pop Pop: Brooks, you are becoming Pop Pop's little man. Voom, voom, and around, and around we go.

Brooks: I love it when you bounce me off your knee, and especially when we play like I'm an airplane. You sure know how to have fun.

Pop Pop: Yep. We have BIG fun. You remind me of your mother when she was a little girl. Look at that smile; that's her alright.

Brooks: Pop Pop, when I see you come into the room, I know that there is going to be some fun games going on. That's why I love coming to your house.

Patience and Pride

Slim: Grand Dad, how am I doing on this new bike that you're teaching me to ride?

Grand Dad: Oh, Slim, you're a fast learner. You are getting the hang of this just as easy as you did basketball.

Slim: You have to watch me more carefully than basketball, just in case I fall.

Grand Dad: Don't worry Slim, it's easier than you think. Just keep trying and NEVER give up!

Slim: I'll be gliding along in no time.

Grand Dad: (I'll have to make myself a note to go out and buy him that protective helmet, kneepads and gloves to let him know it's OK to fall.) Slim, remember, when you fall just dust yourself off and try again!

Grandparents Tell The Best Stories

Grandma Anna: Toney and Jane, I'm so glad you are here to help me with the laundry.

Toney: We like coming to the laundromat with you, Grandma Anna. You always tell us about the old days when the washing was done by hand with just a bucket and a washboard.

Grandma Anna: That's right! Maybe one day I can find an old bucket and washboard and teach you two how to do laundry by hand. What do you think?

Jane: I would like to try that Grandma Anna.

Toney: Me, too! Now that machines have taken over, seeing how to hand wash would be fun. We're glad somebody made washing machines, because when we are here, you have plenty of time to tell us about the old days.

Ironing Things Out

Grandma: Sweet little Angel, while you play, Grandma does her work.

Angel: This is fun! This is fun! I'll give you another one! (That's part of our special song that Grandma and I sing when she's doing ironing. I play in the clothes until she takes the last piece).

Grandma: Angel, Angel, oh so sweet, time with you is such a treat!

Angel: (When I give Grandma the last thing in the basket, I sing real loud), "That is Grandma's very last one, Now we'll go out and have some fun!"

Big Sky Country

Bre Bre: Me and Nita like coming out to the country to visit you Big Momma.

Nita: Lets go sit on the porch and watch the stars. We don't see as many stars in the city as we do when we come out here. I wonder if the moon really has a man in it?

Big Momma: No Nita, it doesn't have a man in it. But there have been astronauts who have visited the moon. Black astronauts like Drs. Mae Jemison and Bernard Harris have had the opportunity to go into outer space.

Nita: I wonder if I'll ever get to go into outer space?

Big Momma: If you study and work hard in school, it's possible.

Big Momma: Do you guys see those set of stars over there?

Bre Bre: Are you talking about those there Big Momma?

Big Momma: No, those over there by the moon. A group of stars collectively form what is called a constellation.

Bre Bre: Oh, I see them; they look like a dipping spoon.

Big Momma: That constellation over there is called the "Big Dipper."

My Sweet Tomato

Granny: Give me a big ol' hug and a kiss. I haven't seen my Sweetie all week long. Would you like to help Granny in the garden?

Tequia: You know I do Granny; I love working in the garden with you. Can we pick those roses over there? I want to surprise Momma when she comes to pick me up.

Granny: That's sure is a nice thing to do for your Mother, Sweetie.

Tequia: Like you always taught me, "Do unto others, as you shall have others do unto you."

Granny: I'm glad to see that I'm rubbing off on you.

A Grandparent's Story:
Jesse E. McGee, M.D.

I was fortunate to have two grandparents, growing up in the small town of Cleveland, Mississippi. We were a very close knit family that maintained an excellent relationship with each other, especially our elders. It was family tradition that every Sunday was Grandparents' Day. We'd visit with them, have a great meal together and hear them share stories of all the great and interesting people from their past. The McGees have a proud family history. We'd gather around and listen to Elizabeth and Lee "Buster" Shorter tell us about their youth — their storied courtship — and the many aunts, uncles, and cousins in their treasured photo album.

There's no love like a grandparent's love. That's immediately evident the moment you see a grandparent interact with their grandchildren. As a young lad, I was my grandparent's main attraction on many of those Sundays. I'd be on Grandpa's knee as he entertained his visitors with story after story. Meanwhile, he'd playfully keep my attention with occasional pokes in the side that drew instant laughter. A grandparent's love expressed in their grandchild's joy is a gift that keeps on giving.

Our old family tradition is relegated to holidays gatherings today. However, our expressions toward one another are a beautiful sight to behold. I am blessed to still have my father, Evage McGee. With faith and love, his direction encouraged me to pursue my dreams and make the family proud. As a cardiologist and advocate for maintaining a healthy heart, I know laughter and exercise are powerful medicines. I've been blessed also to have a grandson, Dylan McGee, age 5. He is already enamoured with the medical profession. And, he'll tell anyone, "Right now, I've already got one patient! It's my great-grandfather. But I'll have more to come!" Dylan is an absolute joy. He spends every other weekend with me and his grandmother, Wilma. He likes to go down to the office and sit in my chair. Then, we go to visit his patient (his great-grandfather), where he takes my stethoscope, and listens to his heart! How wonderful it is to be part of such a rich legacy.

I Will Help You Carry On

Ma Dear: How are you feeling, Mia?

Mia: I'm feeling a little better.

Ma Dear: Let me feel your head, and see if your fever has gone down.

Mia: I think it has gone down just a little bit.

Ma Dear: Let's see what the thermometer reading shows.

Ma Dear: 99 degrees. I see that it has dropped from yesterday's 102.

Mia: What kind of soup did you bring me?

Ma Dear: I brought your favorite, chicken noodle. Here is some orange juice too. It has Vitamin C in it, which is good for you.

Mia: Ma Dear, I'm glad that I have you to nurse me back to health.

Sharing the Wealth

Pa Pa: Come on over here Jahylyn.

Jahylyn: Yeah, Pa Pa. What do you have for me?

Pa Pa: Here is some money for the good grades I heard that you made.

Jahylyn: (Pa Pa always slips me some cash. Now I can go to the store and buy that new glove I saw the other day.)

Pa Pa: Be careful. Don't go spending it all in one place.

Jahylyn: I will. Bye Pa Pa. Oh yeah, thanks for the money!

Another Year, Another Blessing

Grams: I wonder who is having a birthday today?

Jay Jay: It's my B-day Grams!

Ivory: How old are you today Jay Jay?

Jay Jay: I'm six years old today. I've almost caught up with you Ivory.

Ivory: Not quite yet!

Jay Jay: Hey Grams, will you tell us a joke?

Ivory: Come on Grams, tell us a good one!

Grams: OK you two. Knock knock.

Ivory & Jay Jay: Who's There?

Grams: Wanda.

Ivory & Jay Jay: Wanda Who?

Grams: *Wanda wish You a* "HAPPY BIRTHDAY!"

Ivory: Grams that was a good one.

Jay Jay: You always tell the funniest jokes. How did you become so funny?

Grams: It comes with age, my children.

Paul Harvey Writes:

We tried so hard to make things better for our kids that we made them worse. For my grandchildren, I'd like better.

I'd really like for them to know about hand me down clothes and homemade ice cream and leftover meat loaf sandwiches. I really would.

I hope you learn humility by being humiliated, and that you learn honesty by being cheated.

I hope you learn to make your own bed and mow the lawn and wash the car.

And I really hope nobody gives you a brand new car when you are sixteen.

It will be good if at least one time you can see puppies born and your old dog put to sleep.

I hope you get a black eye fighting for something you believe in.

I hope you have to share a bedroom with your younger brother/sister. And it's all right if you have to draw a line down the middle of the room, but when he wants to crawl under the covers with you because he's scared, I hope you let him.

When you want to see a movie and your little brother/sister wants to tag along, I hope you'll let him/her.

I hope you have to walk uphill to school with your friends and that you live in a town where you can do it safely.

On rainy days when you have to catch a ride, I hope you don't ask your driver to drop you two blocks away so you won't be seen riding with someone as uncool as your Mom.

If you want a slingshot, I hope your Dad teaches you how to make one instead of buying one.

I hope you learn to dig in the dirt and read books.

When you learn to use computers, I hope you also learn to add and subtract in your head.

I hope you get teased by your friends when you have your first crush on a boy/girl, and when you talk back to your mother that you learn what ivory soap tastes like.

May you skin your knee climbing a mountain, burn your hand on a stove and stick your tongue on a frozen flagpole.

I don't care if you try a beer once, but I hope you don't like it. And if a friend offers you dope or a joint, I hope you realize he is not your friend.

I sure hope you make time to sit on a porch with your Grandma/Grandpa and go fishing with your Uncle.

May you feel sorrow at a funeral and joy during the holidays.

I hope your mother punishes you when you throw a baseball through your neighbor's window and that she hugs you and kisses you at Hannukah/ Christmas time when you give her a plaster mold of your hand.

These things I wish for you - tough times and disappointment, hard work and happiness. To me, it's the only way to appreciate life.

Written with a pen. Sealed with a kiss. I'm here for you. And if I die before you do, I'll go to heaven and wait for you.

Paul Harvey is one of the foremost newsmen and commentators in the business. His nationally syndicated radio program is heard daily on ABC Radio Stations across the country.

Your Personal
Grandparent and Grandchildren Photographs
go here.

Your Personal
Grandparent and Grandchildren Photographs
go here.

Contributor

Paul Underwood, M.D.

Dr. Paul Underwood, President of the Association of Black Cardiologists, Inc., is an interventional cardiologist at North Phoenix Heart Center in Phoenix, AZ. He earned his medical degree and completed his residency at the Mayo Clinic in Rochester, MN. His residency was preceded by a year internship at the Henry Ford Hospital in Detroit, MI. Dr. Underwood's cardiology fellowship was at the Cleveland Clinic in Ohio, followed by an interventional fellowship with the Iowa Heart Center in Des Moines, IA. He is board-certified in internal medicine and cardiovascular diseases, and is a fellow of the American College of Cardiology and the Society of Cardiac Angiography and Intervention.

His research interests encompass various aspects of interventional and clinical cardiology. He has been an investigator in numerous clinical trials, including the ARIES trial of rosuvastatin and atorvastatin in hyperlipidemia and the African American Heart Failure Trial. He's also active with the American Heart Association and is currently the Chairperson of the Cultural Health Initiatives Program of the Arizona affiliate. Dr. Underwood has co-authored many publications focusing on interventional cardiology and heart failure management. He recently authored the chapter, "Covered Stents in Peripheral Vascular Diseases," in the Textbook of Vascular Stenting Interventions.

Dr. Underwood and his wife, Dr. Hollis Underwood, are the proud parents of three children (Paul, III, Ian and Neal).

Contributor

B. Waine Kong, Ph.D., J.D.

As the CEO of the ABC for eighteen years, Dr. Kong is a lawyer as well as educational psychologist. He was Director of the Urban Cardiology Research Center in Baltimore, an Assistant Professor of Human Development at the University of the District of Columbia and Director of Research and Grants at Provident Hospital before assuming his present responsibilities with the ABC.

Between 1979 and 1982, Dr. Kong and Dr. Elijah Saunders, conducted the first clinical trials for African Americans, as well as pioneered the organization of churches and barbershops as high blood pressure control centers with a grant from the National Heart Lung and Blood Institute. He then assisted in the development of similar programs in twenty other cities and won the "Program of the Year" award from Delta Sigma Theta, as well as leadership awards from the Consortium for Southeastern Hypertension Control (COSEHC), and the Health and Welfare Council of Maryland.

In 1982, he was declared the "Father of Church Blood Pressure Control Programs" by the Maryland Association of Blood Pressure Measurement Specialists. In 1986, he won the prestigious community service award at the International Conference on High Blood Pressure Control in Black Populations (ISHIB) held at Emory University for his role in the development of innovative programs to combat cardiovascular diseases in African Americans. He is the author of the Vital Signs Quality of Life Questionnaire.

He has published widely and made presentations in Egypt, Slovenia, Italy, Israel, Jamaica, the Virgin Islands, the Soviet Union, Zimbabwe, Cameroon, South Africa and Kenya about such topics as "Churches as High Blood Pressure Control Centers," "The Underlying Causes of Hypertension in Blacks," "Clinical Drug Trials in Underdeveloped Countries," "Legal Risk Management," and "The History of the Treatment of High Blood Pressure in the United States," "Quality of Life: Is It Just Another Clinical Sign?" and "Who Owns Cultural Property?"

Dr. Kong is a Deacon at Providence Missionary Baptist Church of Atlanta, GA and is a life member of the Alpha Phi Alpha Fraternity, Inc. He is married to Dr. Stephanie Kong, and they have the pleasure of being parents to four children (Jillian, Freddie, Melanie and Aleron) and three grandchildren (MacKenzie, Brooks and Audrey).

Contributor

Jesse E. McGee, MD

Dr. McGee is Chairman of the Board of Directors of the Association of Black Cardiologists, Inc. A thirty year veteran Cardiology and Internal Medicine practitioner, professor and researcher, he is currently Clinical Associate Professor at the University of Tennessee Center for the Health Sciences, Memphis, TN. As a celebrated cardiovascular researcher, he is board-certified in internal medicine and cardiovascular diseases, and is a fellow of the American College of Cardiology. Dr. McGee has contributed to published studies in the American Journal of Cardiology, the Journal of the National Medical Association and the New England Journal of Medicine.

A native of Cleveland, Mississippi, he earned an undergraduate degree from Alcorn State University (1968), a graduate medical degree from the University of Iowa (1974), served an internship and residency at Cleveland-Metropolitan General Hospital (1974-1977), and was appointed Chief Resident at Cleveland-Metropolitan General Hospital in 1977. He is a member of the American Heart Association, the American College of Physicians, the National Medical Association, and serves as president of the Volunteer State Medical Association. He and his lovely wife, Wilma, are the proud parents of two children and the grandparents of one, Dylan McGee, a future cardiologist.

Contributor

Joel Gresham

Joe Gresham, artist, author, and inventor, was born in Ft. Lauderdale, Florida. He received his art training at the Atlanta University Center. His remarkable gift as a painter and watercolorist has brought him significant acclaim. He has been featured in more than 21 solo exhibits, and 29 group exhibits. Joel's artwork has been used in TV sets for popular sitcom shows, and he has received credit for artwork in books in addition to other special promotions. As a three dimensional artist he has crafted award-winning designs for corporate, music and television personalities.

His works are in many public and private collections including Oprah Winfrey, Edwin Moses, Bernie Marcus, Rudolph W. Giuliani, Sam Massell, Buckhead Coalition, Robert Gillaume, Paul Winfield, Marla Gibbs, Winnie Mandela, Muhammad Ali, Hank Aaron, James Worthy, Marquis Grissom, and Quincy Jones.

"As an artist, I've discovered that maintaining strong fundamentals in my art allowed me to develop my own unique style. I capture symmetry and harmonic balance of line and movement, by reinforcing basic principles and communicating their close relationships to life."

"It has been an honor and a distinct pleasure to have collaborated with the Association of Black Cardiologists, Inc. in creating the illustrations in this very valuable resource book. Anyone who reads this book will immediately reflect on fond memories of time spent with those amazingly interesting grandparents in their own lives, who shared so much unconditional love. I recall my own grandmother with whom I developed a wonderful bond during my annual trips to Atlanta as a youth. I believe I inherited her attention to detail as she displayed such dedication to maintaining her garden and her home. She encouraged me to pursue my passion and to express the beauty and sensitivity of my people. I carry her memory close to my heart as I create, reflect and share the beauty of a marvelous people."

Contributor

LaTrese D. Coyt

LaTrese Coyt is the Public Relations/Special Events Manager for the Association of Black Cardiologists, Inc. In this capacity, she functions as the liaison between the ABC and the media, as well as the membership to promote the mission and goals of the organization.

Ms. Coyt is the staff editor of the ABC's quarterly newsletter and assists with the development of the Annual Report and the Pioneering African-Americans in Conquest of Heart Disease calendar. She served as Producer of "Heart Time with the Association of Black Cardiologists" on Atlanta's WCLK promoting the ABC's 7 Steps to Good Health and is also responsible for organizing special events including the ABC's Annual New Year's Eve Symposium/ Celebration which took them to South Africa in 2001.

A native of Canton, Ohio, Ms. Coyt received her Bachelor of Science degree from Ohio University's College of Communications. Additionally, she is a charter member of the nonprofit organization, Teens Conquering Challenges (TCC), a mentor program dedicated to the cultivation and enhancement of minority female teenagers' growth and development. Recognized in the 2003 and 2004 editions of "Who's Who in Black Atlanta," LaTrese and her husband Todd are the proud parents of two children, Morgan and Marcus.

Contributor

Rondereo D. Sidney

Rondereo Sidney is a native of Meridian, Mississippi. He is a graduate of The University of Southern Mississippi (Hattiesburg, MS), where he received a Bachelor of Science degree in Psychology. Upon completing his studies, he relocated to his current home in Atlanta, Georgia.

Mr. Sidney currently works in the Member Services Department for the Association of Black Cardiologists, Inc. (Atlanta, GA) where some of his responsibilities include member recruitment, exhibition at various conferences and symposiums, database management, coordination of ABC's Cardiologist-In-Training program, and ABCDOCS portal maintenance. Prior to transitioning to his current position in the Member Services Department, he played an important role in the Office of Development developing and implementing fund-raising initiatives for ABC's ongoing Capital Campaign, "Building a Healthy Future." He is also the author of the article "Why African American Men Don't Go to the Doctor." Mr. Sidney was honored as the 2003-2004 ABC Employee of the Year.

Prior to joining the ABC family, Mr. Sidney worked at Creative Counseling Services (Atlanta, GA), where he counseled and mentored troubled children referred from Georgia's Department of Family and Children's Services (DFCS). In addition to those responsibilities, he also assisted the parents of the referred DFCS children with obtaining needed assistance.

He prides himself on being a person that believes that for every dark day there is a brighter day ahead, so look to that brighter day. During his leisure time he enjoys traveling, reading, spending time with his family, watching and playing sports.

His parents reside in Meridian, as well as his sister and brother. Great inspiration and material for this book comes from his 5 nieces and nephews (Deseana, Jeremy, Mia, Mark'Kel, and Ke'Shaun).

The Association of Black Cardiologists, Inc.

The ABC was founded in 1974 to bring special attention to the adverse impact of cardiovascular disease on African Americans. We are an inclusive organization, with membership open to everyone who is interested in assuring that African American children know their grandparents so they will become GREAT grandparents themselves. This will only be achieved by lowering the high rate of heart disease, diabetes and stroke in the African American community through:

- Culturally competent health care providers
- Equal access to medical care and innovative technologies
- Effective collaboration with industry, government, professional organizations, and individuals

You can help by volunteering and supporting the following ABC programs:

- Public health education and promotion
- Blood pressure, diabetes, cholesterol, and arrhythmia screenings
- Community health fairs and physical fitness programs (Sweating With The Sisters)
- Youth mentoring programs for careers in science and medicine
- Diet and Nutrition Classes

Other ABC Consumer Education Publications

Books and Brochures

- *A Minute for Your Health*
- *African American Guide to Clinical Trials*
- *Heart Disease and Stroke in African Americans: A Patient Guide*
- *Pioneers in Conquest of Cardiovascular Disease:* A 15 Month Calendar
- *The ABC Spelling Bee Study Guide*
- *Cardiovascular Disease in African American Women:*

RESOURCES

The American College of Cardiology
Heart House
9111 Old Georgetown Road
Bethesda, MD 20814-1699
1-800-253-4636, ext. 694 or 1-301-879-5400
FAX: 1-301-897-9745
www.acc.org

American Diabetes Association (ADA)
1660 Duke Street
Alexandria, VA 22314
1-703-549-1500 1-800-DIABETES www.diabetes.org
ADA publishes The Diabetes Food and Nutrition Bible ($18.95), a handy new guide to healthy food planning, shopping, cooking, and eating.

American Dietetic Association
120 South Riverside Plaza, Suite 2000 Chicago, IL 60606-6995
1-800-877-1600
www.eatright.org

American Heart Association
7272 Greenville Avenue
Dallas, TX 75231-4596
1 -800-242-8721 www.americanheart.org
Ask for "High Blood Pressure in African Americans" and other free publications about heart disease and related health matters.

American Kidney Fund
6110 Executive Boulevard
Rockville, MD 20852
1-800-638-8299 www.kidneyfund.org
Ask for the free brochure, "African Americans and High Blood Pressure."

American Stroke Association, a division of the American Heart Association
1-888-4STROKE (1-888-478-7653)
www.StrokeAssociation.org

Association of Black Psychologists
P.O. Box 55999
Washington, DC 20040-0808
1-202-722-0808
www.abpsi.org

Caloric Control Council
P.O. Box 420187
Atlanta, GA 30342
www.caloriecontrol.org
Offers free information on weight control, diet, and exercise.

Centers for Disease Control and Prevention (CDC)
1600 Clifton Road
Atlanta, GA 30333
1-404-639-3311 or 1-800-311-3435
www.cdc.gov

National Center for Nutrition and Dietetics Information
1-800-366-1655 www.eatright.org
Provides nutrition information and referrals to local registered dietitians.

National Heart, Lung, and Blood Institute
NHLBI Information Center
P.O. Box 30105
Bethesda, MD 20824-0105
301-592-8573
www.nhlbi.nih.gov
E-mail health-related questions and requests to: NHLBIinfo@rover.nhlbi.nih.gov.

National Diabetes Information Clearinghouse (NDIC)
1 Information Way
Bethesda, MD 20892
1-301-654-3327 or 1-800-860-8747
www.niddk.nih.gov
Free publications include "Diabetes in Black Americans" and "Sisters Together," which provides information on weight control for African American women.

National Medical Association
1012 10th Street, NW
Washington, DC 20001-4492
1-202-347-1895 1-888-662-7497
You can ask for referrals to African American physicians in your local area.

National Stroke Association
9707 E. Easter Lane
Englewood, C0 80112
1-800-STROKES 1-303-649-9299

CHILDREN SHOULD KNOW THEIR GRANDPARENTS SO THEY WILL BECOME GREAT GRANDPARENTS

The Association of Black Cardiologists, Inc. (ABC) is the preeminent authority on cardiovascular disease (CVD) prevention in African Americans, and other high risk populations. As the (ABC) celebrates thirty years of collaborative research and service, it presents *Why Grandchildren Should Know Their Grandparents,* their new, innovative cross-generational keepsake. If we are ever going to solve our social problems, we need grandparents to live longer, healthier lives, and to be available to their grandchildren. Think of a community free of juvenile delinquency, adolescent and unwanted pregnancies, school dropouts and underachievement. Such a community is closer to reality where the influence of grandparents is present in young people's lives. A child is only a grandparent away from developing into a happy, well adjusted, contributing member of society. Children readily defy their parents, but they think twice about upsetting grandma or grandpa. There's authority that children respect.

Grandchildren are also fun. In fact, one grandparent said if she knew that grandchildren were going to be so much fun, she would have had them first. This is your legacy and your immortality. After all is said and done, what we leave behind are our children. So, treat them well. Tell them the stories. Teach them to pray and to be respectful. Just be sure you continue to be available to them.

"The grandparent's program with the Association of Black Cardiologists is a tremendous program that brings awareness to the problems of cardiovascular disease in minority populations. Obviously, the disparity in life expectancy as it pertains to blacks compared to whites is unconscionable in this present-day society. I think this initiative will prompt black individuals to pay more attention to healthy lifestyles and the importance of building the bridges between the health community and the consumer community to increase life expectancy in our community."

Dr. Winston Price, President
The National Medical Association

"In a world where everyone is too busy, TV personality Willard Scott says the best thing grandparents can give their grandchildren is time—time to love and be loved, time to share, and time to listen, really, really listen. Children like to be listened to, need to be listened to. Sadly, that doesn't happen as often as it should. Grandparents can fill that void and learn a lot about their grandchildren at the same time. It's an opportunity to be wise, to be nurturing, to teach and be taught."

AARP Grandparent Information Center
Washington, D.C.